W9-DDK-472

INSIDE THE NBA

WASHINGTON WIZARDS

Sam Moussavi and Samantha Nugent

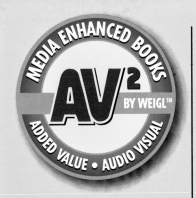

AV² provides enriched content that supplements and complements this book. Weigl's AV² books strive to create inspired learning and engage young minds in a total learning experience.

Your AV² Media Enhanced books come alive with...

Audio
Listen to sections of the book read aloud.

Key Words
Study vocabulary, and complete a matching word activity.

Video
Watch informative video clips.

Quizzes
Test your knowledge.

Embedded Weblinks
Gain additional information for research.

Slide Show
View images and captions, and prepare a presentation.

Try This!
Complete activities and hands-on experiments.

... and much, much more!

Go to www.av2books.com, and enter this book's unique code.

BOOK CODE

Q875327

AV² by Weigl brings you media enhanced books that support active learning.

Published by AV² by Weigl
350 5th Avenue, 59th Floor
New York, NY 10118
Website: www.av2books.com

Library of Congress Control Number: 2016935125

ISBN 978-1-4896-4729-0 (hardcover)
ISBN 978-1-4896-4730-6 (multi-user eBook)

Printed in the United States of America in Brainerd, Minnesota
1 2 3 4 5 6 7 8 9 0 20 19 18 17 16

082016
200516

Project Coordinator Heather Kissock
Art Director Terry Paulhus

Photo Credits
Every reasonable effort has been made to trace ownership and to obtain permission to reprint copyright material. The publishers would be pleased to have any errors or omissions brought to their attention so that they may be corrected in subsequent printings.

Weigl acknowledges NewsCom, Getty Images, and Alamy as its primary image suppliers for this title.

WASHINGTON WIZARDS

CONTENTS

Introduction

It did not take long for the Wizards **franchise** to become competitive after joining the NBA in 1961. Known then as the Baltimore Bullets, the team made the **playoffs** in just its fourth season. The 1970s were even more successful for the franchise. The Bullets made four **NBA Finals** appearances between 1971 and 1979, winning their one and only NBA title in 1978.

Although the team never won more than 43 games in the 1980s, the Wizards made the playoffs seven times in the decade. The Bullets missed the playoffs in 1981, breaking a 12-year postseason streak. Washington made it past the first round once in 1982.

Forward Markieff Morris was traded to the Washington Wizards from the Phoenix Suns in 2016.

After making the playoffs in 20 of its first 25 seasons, the franchise struggled for much of the 1990s. A name change to the Washington Wizards in 1997 did little to help the team win. Even though the Wizards made four playoff appearances in the mid-2000s, the team struggled to find consistency. The Wizards are now led by superstar John Wall. The team's back-to-back appearances in the Eastern **Conference** Playoffs give Wizards fans hope for the future.

Center Nene Hilario started playing basketball in his home country of Brazil. He was drafted by the Denver Nuggets in 2002 and was traded to the Washington Wizards in 2012.

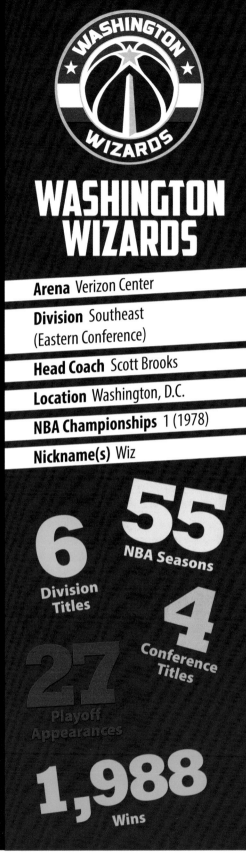

WASHINGTON WIZARDS

Arena Verizon Center

Division Southeast (Eastern Conference)

Head Coach Scott Brooks

Location Washington, D.C.

NBA Championships 1 (1978)

Nickname(s) Wiz

6 Division Titles

55 NBA Seasons

4 Conference Titles

27 Playoff Appearances

1,988 Wins

History

After drafting Wes Unseld in the 1968 draft, the Washington Bullets went from 36 wins the previous season to 57 wins.

The Wizards franchise has retired **4** players' jerseys in its history.

The Wizards franchise joined the NBA as the Chicago Packers in 1961. The team changed its name to the Chicago Zephyrs before the 1962–63 season. After two seasons in Chicago, the team moved to Maryland and became the Baltimore Bullets. In 1965, the Bullets made the NBA Playoffs for the first time in franchise history.

In 1973, the team changed its name again, this time to the Capital Bullets. The following year, the team became known as the Washington Bullets. This name change proved lucky for the team. In 1978, the Washington Bullets won the NBA Finals.

The Bullets struggled in the 1990s. Due to increasing gun violence in Washington, D.C., the team faced pressure to change its name. In 1998, the Bullets became the Wizards. Michael Jordan came out of retirement in 2001 to play for the Washington Wizards, but could not lead the team to the postseason. Washington drafted **point guard** John Wall with the first pick in the 2010 **NBA Draft**. Wall led the team to the second round of the playoffs in 2014 and 2015. The franchise had not been to the second round since 2005.

After coming out of retirement, Michael Jordan played two seasons with the Washington Wizards.

The Arena

The Verizon Center is nicknamed the "Phone Booth" because of Verizon's association with telecommunication and cell phones.

Verizon Center is the 4th largest arena in the NBA.

When the franchise was located in Chicago from 1961 to 1963, its home games were played at two different arenas. The Packers first played at the International Amphitheatre and then at the Chicago Coliseum. Both arenas were located in downtown Chicago.

After the franchise moved to Baltimore and became the Bullets, the team moved into Baltimore Civic Center. The Bullets stayed there from 1963 to 1973. The franchise made its first playoff appearance as well as its first NBA Finals appearance while playing at Baltimore Civic Center.

In 1973, the Washington Bullets moved to the Capital Centre in Landover, Maryland, a suburb of Washington, D.C. In 1978, the Bullets won their only NBA Championship while playing at the Capital Centre. When the team changed its name to "Wizards" in 1997, it also moved into a downtown Washington, D.C. arena called the Verizon Center. The arena is situated in the Chinatown District, and it is where the Wizards currently play all of their home games.

Sometimes, fans at the Verizon Center receive commemorative towels or t-shirts before home games.

Where They Play

British Columbia
Alberta
Ontario
Saskatchewan
Manitoba
CAN
Washington
9 Oregon
Montana
North Dakota
Minnesota **7**
Wisconsin
25
Idaho
South Dakota
Iowa **21**
5
Wyoming
Nebraska
Illinois
Nevada
10
Utah
Colorado
6
Kansas
Missouri
1
California
2
8 Oklahoma
13
Arizona
Arkansas
3
New Mexico
4
11
Pacific Ocean
Texas
Louisiana
15
12 Gulf of Mexico
MEXICO

NBA WESTERN CONFERENCE

PACIFIC DIVISION	NORTHWEST DIVISION	SOUTHWEST DIVISION
1. Golden State Warriors	6. Denver Nuggets	11. Dallas Mavericks
2. Los Angeles Clippers	7. Minnesota Timberwolves	12. Houston Rockets
3. Los Angeles Lakers	8. Oklahoma City Thunder	13. Memphis Grizzlies
4. Phoenix Suns	9. Portland Trail Blazers	14. New Orleans Pelicans
5. Sacramento Kings	10. Utah Jazz	15. San Antonio Spurs

Verizon Center

Arena
Verizon Center

Location
601 F Street NW
Washington, D.C. 20004

Broke Ground
October 18, 1995

Completed
December 2, 1997

Features
- Seats 20,356
- Metro-Rail Access
- 106 Luxury Suites

LEGEND
☆ Verizon Center
■ Western Conference
■ Eastern Conference

Verizon Center,
Washington, D.C.

Atlantic
Ocean

SOUTHEAST DIVISION	CENTRAL DIVISION	ATLANTIC DIVISION
16. Atlanta Hawks	21. Chicago Bulls	26. Boston Celtics
17. Charlotte Hornets	22. Cleveland Cavaliers	27. Brooklyn Nets
18. Miami Heat	23. Detroit Pistons	28. New York Knicks
19. Orlando Magic	24. Indiana Pacers	29. Philadelphia 76ers
★ 20. Washington Wizards	25. Milwaukee Bucks	30. Toronto Raptors

The Uniforms

1

The Wizards played six games in their **"Baltimore Pride"** uniforms during the 2015–16 season.

In 2011, Adidas designed the modern color block uniforms. These are the uniforms still worn today.

When the franchise moved to Baltimore in 1963, its colors were navy blue and orange. The home uniforms were white with orange trim. The away uniforms were navy blue with orange trim. Both uniforms read "Bullets." The team changed its colors to red, white, and blue before the 1969–70 season. From 1969 to 1973, the Baltimore Bullets had white home uniforms and red away uniforms.

The team chose to completely change its uniforms after the name change to the Washington Wizards. In 1997, the colors became blue, black, and gold. The home uniforms were white, and the away uniforms were blue. Both uniforms read "Wizards." In 2011, the Wizards returned to the red, white, and navy blue color scheme as was worn during the Bullets era. Today, the Wizards have kept this color scheme, but have redesigned their uniforms yet again. This time, they have gone with a simple design, featuring red uniforms with "Washington" across the chest while away, and white uniforms with "Wizards" across the chest while playing at home.

 The blue uniforms worn between 1997 and 2010 were made by Champion.

AWAY

The Coaches

 Before becoming a head coach, Brooks was a professional basketball player. He began his coaching career in 2000 as an assistant coach with the Los Angeles Stars.

The Wizards **won** **46 games** during previous coach Randy Wittman's fourth season in 2014–15.

The Wizards franchise has had 23 head coaches over the course of 55 seasons in the NBA. Ten of the head coaches led the team to the NBA Playoffs, for a total of 27 postseason appearances. Three of the coaches, K.C. Jones, Gene Shue, and Dick Motta, led the team to four NBA Finals appearances. Former NBA players Eddie Jordan, Doug Collins, and Darrell Walker have also served as coaches for the franchise.

GENE SHUE Gene Shue coached the Baltimore Bullets from 1967 to 1973, and then coached the Washington Bullets from 1980 to 1986. In Shue's 12 seasons with the franchise, he led the team to nine playoff appearances. He is the Bullets' all-time leader in regular season coaching wins, at 522. Shue also won 19 games in the playoffs.

DICK MOTTA Dick Motta coached the Washington Bullets for four seasons, from 1976 to 1980. The Bullets made the playoffs in each of Motta's four seasons. The Bullets made two straight NBA Finals appearances in 1978 and 1979. Washington won the 1978 NBA Finals, and Motta remains the only coach to lead the franchise to a title.

SCOTT BROOKS Scott Brooks was named head coach of the Washington Wizards on April 27, 2016. Brooks was the head coach of the Oklahoma City Thunder (OKC) from 2008 to 2015. Brooks led OKC to five playoff appearances, including the 2012 NBA Finals. This was the franchise's first finals appearance since moving to Oklahoma City. In seven seasons as Thunder coach, he won 338 regular season games and another 39 in the playoffs.

The Mascots

G-Wiz's favorite physical activities are jumping jacks, push-ups, and dancing to entertain the crowd.

The Washington Wizards have two official mascots. One of them is G-Wiz, a blue and red wizard that wears a magician's hat and a Wizards jersey. The other one is G-Man, a slam-dunking superhero dressed in blue spandex. G-Wiz became the team's mascot in 1997, and G-Man joined him shortly after.

G-Wiz and G-Man can be seen at every Wizards home game at Verizon Center. Both mascots entertain Wizards fans during timeouts and halftime. G-Wiz does funny pranks, and G-Man does acrobatic, high-flying dunk routines. G-Wiz and G-Man can also be seen around the nation's capital at team charity events and school pep rallies.

fun facts

#1 G-Man only appears during home games at the fourth quarter, when the players need energy from the fans the most.

#2 G-Wiz wanted to be a "Wizards Girl," a member of the team's cheerleading squad. When he did not make the squad, he became a mascot instead.

Superstars

Many great players have suited up for the Wizards. A few of them have become icons of the team and the city it represents.

Gus Johnson

The Baltimore Bullets selected forward Gus Johnson with the tenth overall pick in the 1963 NBA Draft. Johnson played in Baltimore for nine seasons, from 1963 to 1972. He averaged 17 points, 13 rebounds, and 2 **assists** per game with the Bullets. Johnson made five All-Star teams and five postseason appearances with Baltimore. He made the NBA All-Defensive First Team in 1970 and 1971. Johnson also won an American Basketball Association (ABA) Championship with the Indiana Pacers in 1973. He entered the Basketball Hall of Fame in 2010.

Position: Forward/Center
NBA Seasons: 10 (1963–1973)
Born: December 13, 1938, Akron, Ohio

Elvin Hayes

Elvin Hayes joined the Baltimore Bullets in a trade from the Houston Rockets before the 1972–73 season. Hayes played with the franchise for nine seasons in both Baltimore and Washington. He was a member of the 1978 NBA Champion Washington Bullets. Hayes averaged 21 points, 12 rebounds, and 2 **blocks** per game during his time with the Bullets. He made eight All-Star appearances with the franchise. Hayes was inducted into the Basketball Hall of Fame in 1990.

Position: Center/Power Forward
NBA Seasons: 16 (1968–1984)
Born: November 17, 1945, Rayville, Louisiana

Gilbert Arenas

Gilbert Arenas signed with the Washington Wizards as a **free agent** before the 2003–04 season. He played in Washington from 2003 to 2011. Arenas became one of the NBA's most explosive scorers with the Wizards. He averaged 25 points a game across his eight seasons in Washington. He set the franchise record for most points in a game with 60 in 2006. Arenas led the Wizards to the playoffs three times and made three All-Star teams. He is also the franchise leader in most **three-pointers** made, with 868.

Position: Point Guard
NBA Seasons: 11 (2001–2012)
Born: January 6, 1982, Tampa, Florida

John Wall

The Wizards selected point guard John Wall out of the University of Kentucky with the first overall pick in the 2010 NBA Draft. Wall is currently Washington's best player and one of the fastest players in the league. He has made three NBA All-Star teams from 2014 to 2016. In six seasons as a member of the Washington Wizards, Wall has averaged 17 points, 8 assists, and 4 rebounds per game. He led the team to two straight NBA Playoff appearances in 2014 and 2015.

Position: Point Guard
NBA Seasons: 6 (2010–present)
Born: September 6, 1990, Raleigh, North Carolina

The Greatest of All Time

There are several standout players on the Wizards roster who have worked hard to push the team to success. Often, there is one player who has become known as the "Greatest of All Time," or GOAT. This player has gone above and beyond to achieve greatness and to help his team shine.

Wes Unseld

Position: Center/Power Forward • **NBA Seasons:** 13 (1968–1981)
Born: March 14, 1946, Louisville, Kentucky

Wes Unseld was selected by the Baltimore Bullets with the second overall pick in the 1968 NBA Draft. Unseld spent his entire 13-season NBA career with the Baltimore and Washington Bullets. He was a member of the team during the 1978 NBA Finals win and received the Finals' MVP Award for his work in the series. Unseld was also a part of the franchise's other Finals appearances in 1971, 1975, and 1979.

He won the NBA's MVP Award in 1979 and made five NBA All-Star teams as a member of the Bullets. Unseld finished his career with averages of 10 points, 14 rebounds, and 3 assists per game. He retired from the Bullets and the NBA after the 1980–81 season. Unseld was inducted into the Basketball Hall of Fame in 1988.

During the 1969–70 season, Unseld scored a total of 526 points.

From 1979 to 1980, Unseld made 366 assists. That was his second highest assist record for a season.

fun facts

#1 Wes Unseld was voted NBA Most Valuable Player in 1969.

#2 He was included on five NBA All-Star Teams.

#3 Unseld had 12 NBA Playoff appearances during his career.

#4 He had 13,769 career rebounds.

Wes Unseld was honored on the court at the Verizon Center in 2013. The event commemorated the 35th anniversary of the only championship in franchise history.

The Moment

During the 1978 NBA Playoffs and Finals, small forward Kevin Grevey played an average of 27.8 minutes per game.

The greatest moment in Wizards history came during the 1978 NBA Finals, when the team was known as the Washington Bullets. The Bullets had been to the Finals twice before in the 1970s, but were swept both times. The championship in 1978 put the Bullets against the Seattle SuperSonics. The Bullets were led by Wes Unseld and Elvin Hayes, along with head coach Dick Motta.

The Bullets came into the 1978 Finals as underdogs, and the Sonics and Bullets split the first four games of the series. In game 5, the SuperSonics won, sending the Bullets home facing possible elimination. Back in Maryland, the Bullets beat Seattle in game 6 to tie the series. The series would go back to Seattle for the deciding game 7.

Early in game 7, the Bullets took control. It was not until the fourth quarter that Seattle tightened the score. With 30 seconds left and Washington up by only two points, Unseld made two free throws to put the game out of reach for Seattle. The Bullets won their first and only NBA Championship with the game 7 win in Seattle.

Wes Unseld was known as a fierce rebounder and excellent defensive player. He used both of these skills to bring home the NBA Championship victory.

The owner of the Bullets, and later the Wizards, Abe Pollin, is the only owner in the history of the franchise to boast a championship win.

All-Time Records

801

Most Assists in a Season
Wizards point guard Rod Strickland handed out a franchise single-season record 801 assists during the 1997–98 season.

397

372

Most Offensive Rebounds in a Season
Bullets center Moses Malone pulled down a single-season record 372 **offensive rebounds** during the 1987–88 season.

52%

Most Blocks in a Season
Washington Bullets center Manute Bol had a single-season record 397 blocks during the 1985–86 season.

178 Most Steals in a Season
Washington Bullets point guard Gus Williams finished the 1984–85 seasons with a single-season record 178 **steals**.

Highest Three Point Field Goal Percentage in a Season
Washington Bullets **sharpshooter** Tim Legler made a single-season record 52 percent of his three pointers during the 1995–96 season.

60% Highest Field Goal Percentage in a Season
Bullets center Gheorghe Muresan holds the single-season record for highest **field goal** percentage, at 60 percent in 1996–97.

Timeline

Throughout the team's history, the Wizards have had many memorable events that have become defining moments for the team and its fans.

1961–1963

In 1961, the franchise joins the NBA as the Chicago Packers. After one season as the Packers, the team changes its name to the Chicago Zephyrs.

1970–1971

Led by coach Gene Shue and Unseld, the Bullets make it to the NBA Finals for the first time in franchise history.

1960

1970

1980

1963

The franchise moves to Baltimore after two seasons in Chicago and changes its name to the Bullets. The Baltimore Bullets win 31 games during the 1963–64 season.

1974–1975

The team changes its name to the Washington Bullets and wins 60 games during the 1974–75 season.

1964–1965

The Bullets make the playoffs for the first time in franchise history in 1965.

1997

The team changes its name to the Washington Wizards. The name change coincides with the team moving into a brand new arena in downtown Washington, D.C.

The Future

The Wizards are looking to build on recent success and climb to the top of the Eastern Conference. The team is led by guards John Wall and Bradley Beal. Wall's speed and ability to hand out assists are huge benefits for the team. Beal's ability to score is also key for the team.

1973–1974

The franchise moves to Landover, Maryland, a suburb of Washington, D.C. The team is known as the Capital Bullets for the 1973–74 season.

2001–2003

NBA legend Michael Jordan comes out of retirement and plays two seasons for the Washington Wizards.

| 1990 | 2000 | 2010 | 2020 |

1979

Washington makes it back to the NBA Finals for the second year in a row. The team loses the 1979 Finals series to the SuperSonics. The franchise is the only one in the NBA to play in the Finals four times in the 1970s.

1978

Led by Unseld, Hayes, and forward Bob Dandridge, the Bullets defeated the Seattle SuperSonics in the 1978 NBA Finals. The championship series win represents the franchise's first, and only, NBA title.

2004–2005

The team makes the playoffs as the Wizards for the first time. Washington defeats the Chicago Bulls in the first round of the playoffs four games to two.

Write a Biography

Life Story

A person's life story can be the subject of a book. This kind of book is called a biography. Biographies often describe the lives of people who have achieved great success. These people may be alive today, or they may have lived many years ago. Reading a biography can help you learn more about a great person.

Get the Facts

Use this book, and research in the library and on the internet, to find out more about your favorite Star. Learn as much about this player as you can. What position does he play? What are his statistics in important categories? Has he set any records? Also, be sure to write down key events in the person's life. What was his childhood like? What has he accomplished off the court? Is there anything else that makes this person special or unusual?

Use the Concept Web

A concept web is a useful research tool. Read the questions in the concept web on the following page. Answer the questions in your notebook. Your answers will help you write a biography.

Concept Web

Your Opinion
- What did you learn from the books you read in your research?
- Would you suggest these books to others?
- Was anything missing from these books?

Adulthood
- Where does this individual currently reside?
- Does he or she have a family?

Childhood
- Where and when was this person born?
- Describe his or her parents, siblings, and friends.
- Did this person grow up in unusual circumstances?

Accomplishments off the Court
- What is this person's life's work?
- Has he or she received awards or recognition for accomplishments?
- How have this person's accomplishments served others?

Write a Biography

Help and Obstacles
- Did this individual have a positive attitude?
- Did he or she receive help from others?
- Did this person have a mentor?
- Did this person face any hardships?
- If so, how were the hardships overcome?

Accomplishments on the Court
- What records does this person hold?
- What key games and plays have defined his career?
- What are his stats in categories important to his position?

Work and Preparation
- What was this person's education?
- What was his or her work experience?
- How does this person work?
- What is the process he or she uses?

Trivia Time

Take this quiz to test your knowledge of the Washington Wizards.
The answers are printed upside down under each question.

1 Where do the Wizards currently play their home games?

A. Verizon Center

2 How many assists did Rod Strickland have in 1997–98?

A. 801

3 When did the franchise change its name to the Wizards?

A. 1997

4 In what year was Wes Unseld drafted?

A. 1968

5 How many games did the Baltimore Bullets win in 1974–75?

A. 60

6 When did the franchise move to Baltimore?

A. 1963

7 In which conference do the Wizards play?

A. Eastern Conference

8 What position did Gilbert Arenas play?

A. Point guard

9 When did Michael Jordan play for the Wizards?

A. 2001–2003

10 When did the Wizards draft John Wall?

A. 2010

11 When did the franchise play its first NBA season?

A. 1961

12 How many All-Star appearances did Elvin Hayes make with the franchise?

A. Eight

Key Words

assists: a statistic that is attributed to up to two players of the scoring team who shoot, pass, or deflect the ball toward the scoring teammate

blocks: when a defensive player taps an offensive player's shot out of the air and stops it from getting to the basket

conference: an association of sports teams that play each other

field goal: a basket scored while the clock is running and the ball is in play

franchise: a team that is a member of a professional sports league

free agent: a player who is not under contract and free to sign with any team he or she wishes

NBA Draft: the annual event in June where NBA teams select players from college to join the league

NBA Finals: the last round of the NBA Playoffs, where one team from the Western Conference plays another team from the Eastern Conference and the winner is crowned NBA Champion

offensive rebounds: rebounds secured by an offensive player after his or her teammate misses a shot

playoffs: a series of games that occur after regular season play

point guard: the player who directs the team's offense

sharpshooter: a consistently accurate shooter

steals: to take possession of the ball from the other team

three-pointers: shots that count for three points, taken from behind the three-point line

Index

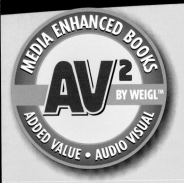

Log on to www.av2books.com

AV² by Weigl brings you media enhanced books that support active learning. Go to www.av2books.com, and enter the special code found on page 2 of this book. You will gain access to enriched and enhanced content that supplements and complements this book. Content includes video, audio, weblinks, quizzes, a slide show, and activities.

AV² Online Navigation

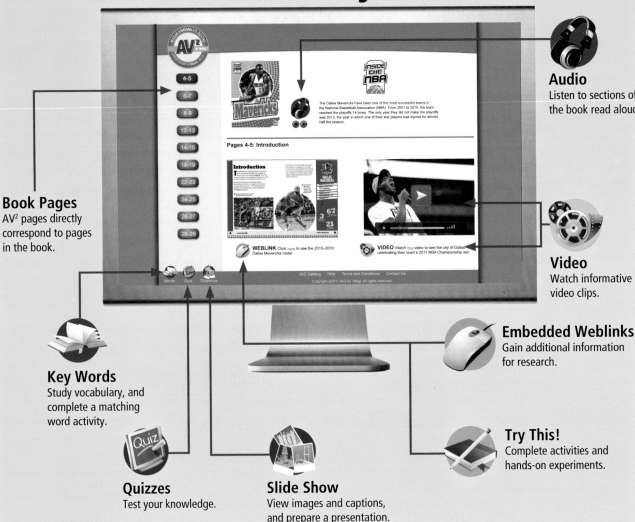

Book Pages
AV² pages directly correspond to pages in the book.

Audio
Listen to sections of the book read aloud

Video
Watch informative video clips.

Embedded Weblinks
Gain additional information for research.

Key Words
Study vocabulary, and complete a matching word activity.

Try This!
Complete activities and hands-on experiments.

Quizzes
Test your knowledge.

Slide Show
View images and captions, and prepare a presentation.

AV² was built to bridge the gap between print and digital. We encourage you to tell us what you like and what you want to see in the future.

Sign up to be an AV² Ambassador at www.av2books.com/ambassador.

Due to the dynamic nature of the Internet, some of the URLs and activities provided as part of AV² by Weigl may have changed or ceased to exist. AV² by Weigl accepts no responsibility for any such changes. All media enhanced books are regularly monitored to update addresses and sites in a timely manner. Contact AV² by Weigl at 1-866-649-3445 or av2books@weigl.com with any questions, comments, or feedback.